Dog]

Facts for Fun!

Book A

By Wyatt Michaels

Copyright 2012

Image courtesy of foto-junky once in a while photography

Which dog breed can jump up to 6 feet high from a sitting position?

A. American Bulldog
B. Alaskan Husky
C. Australian Cattle Dog

Image courtesy of Experience LA

The answer is B. Alaskan Husky

They really don't have springs in their feet.

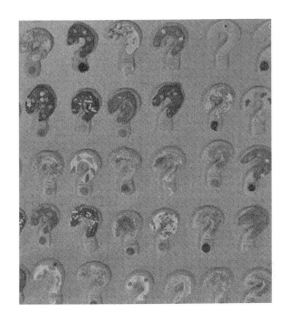

Image courtesy of Scott McLeod

Which breed came to America on the
Mayflower?

A. American Cocker Spaniel
B. Airedale Terrier
C. American Bulldog

Image courtesy of RL Johnson

The answer is A. American Cocker Spaniel

But it probably wasn't called "American" at the time!

Image courtesy of Pepo 13

Which breed was the choice of law
enforcement before German Shepherd?

A. Alaskan Husky

B. Australian Shepherd

C. Airedale Terrier

Image courtesy of Lulu Hoeller

The answer is C. Airedale Terrier

Airedale Terriers were first selected for duty as police dogs in Europe because of their intelligence, good scenting abilities and their hard, wiry coats that were easy to maintain and clean.

Image courtesy of mscaprikell

Which breed is commonly chosen to
work with unusual livestock such as
ducks, geese, and rabbits?

A. Australian Shepherd
B. Australian Cattle Dog
C. American Bulldog

Image courtesy of carterse

The answer is A. Australian Shepherd

They are often chosen because of their ability to adapt to a situation, and think for itself.

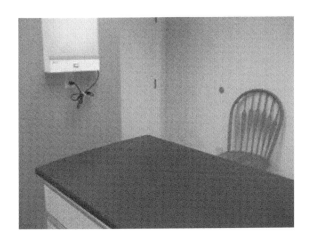

Image courtesy of caterina

Which breed usually has more injuries than illnesses?

A. Alaskan Husky

B. Alaskan Malamute

C. Australian Cattle Dog

Image courtesy of sally9258

The answer is C. Australian Cattle Dog

Due to occupational hazards, these dogs in fact have more injuries than illnesses.

Image courtesy of Nina Matthews Photography

Which breed is an American dog that is used to herd Australian sheep?

A. American Cocker Spaniel
B. Australian Shepherd
C. American Bulldog

Image courtesy of Ted Van Pelt

The answer is B. Australian Shepherd

One theory of how these dogs got their name is the Australian sheep that they were known to herd.

Image courtesy of eliduke

Which breed helped Rear Admiral
Richard Byrd explore the South Pole?

A. American Cocker Spaniel

B. Australian Shepherd

C. Alaskan Malamute

Image courtesy of snapped up

The answer is C. Alaskan Malamute

That was one well-traveled dog, from Alaska to the South Pole!

Image courtesy of Alaskan Dude

Which breed is a sled dog, but not a racing sled dog?

A. Alaskan Husky
B. American Bulldog
C. Alaskan Malamute

Image courtesy of Richard Bartz

The answer is C. Alaskan Malamute

These dogs were used for heavy freighting, pulling supplies to villages and camps in groups of at least 4 dogs for heavy loads.

Image courtesy of C. K. Hartman

Which breed is used to herd cattle long distances over rough terrain?

A. Australian Cattle Dog
B. Alaskan Malamute
C. Australian Shepherd

Image courtesy of zingpix

The answer is A. Australian Cattle Dog

Some believe these dogs are the best in the world for this job.

Image courtesy of Randy Stewart

Which breed did settlers depend on to deal with wild pigs?

A. Australian Cattle Dog
B. American Bulldog
C. Australian Shepherd

Image courtesy of Legal Admin

The answer is B. American Bulldog

While bulldogs were used for many
farm tasks, ranchers especially
appreciated their ability to deal with the
pesky wild pigs.

Image courtesy of dun deagh

Which breed is nicknamed "king of terriers" because it is the largest terrier breed?

A. Australian Terrier

B. Airedale Terrier

C. American Hairless Terrier

Image courtesy of Lulu Hoeller

The answer is B. Airedale Terrier

The other two answers are much smaller
dogs.

Image courtesy of AMagill

The top dogs in which breed sell for $10-15,000?

   A. Airedale Terrier
   B. American Cocker Spaniel
   C. Alaskan Husky

Image courtesy of public domain

The answer is C. Alaskan Husky

This is the price tag for a top-notch racing lead dog.

Image courtesy of purpleslog

Which breed includes Queensland
Heelers, Red Heelers, and Blue Heelers?

A. Airedale Terrier
B. Australian Cattle Dog
C. Alaskan Husky

Image courtesy of doggybytes

The answer is B. Australian Cattle Dog

Queensland Heelers got their name
from Queensland, Australia. Red &
Blue Heelers got their names from the
brown or black hair distributed through
their otherwise white coat, giving them
an appearance of a red or blue dog. The
Heeler name comes from their practice
of nipping at the heels of cattle to get
them to move.

Image courtesy of Civilian Scrabble

Which breed had dogs associated with Presidents Nixon, Truman, and Rutherford B. Hayes?

A. Airedale Terrier
B. American Cocker Spaniel
C. Alaskan Husky

Image courtesy of Mike Baird

The answer is B. American Cocker
Spaniel

Nixon's dog was named Checkers,
Truman's spaniel was named Feller, and
Hayes named his dog Dot.

Image courtesy of Ken Lund

Which breed was used by southern farmers and ranchers as working dogs?

A. Australian Cattle Dog
B. American Bulldog
C. Airedale Terrier

Image courtesy of Kroon78

The answer is B. American Bulldog

Wild pigs were their specialty, but bulldogs were also used as farm guardians, stock dogs, and catch dogs.

Image courtesy of b a r t

Which breed was extremely valuable to miners during the Klondike Gold Rush of 1896?

A. Alaskan Malamute

B. Alaskan Husky

C. American Bulldog

Image courtesy of sirispj

The answer is A. Alaskan Malamute

In contrast to Alaskan Huskies, instead of being a racing dog, Malamutes are working dogs. They have been known to hunt as well as pull heavy freight.

Image courtesy of Christine zenino

Which breed served as search and
rescue dogs in Greenland during World
War II?

A. Australian Cattle Dog
B. Alaskan Malamute
C. Alaskan Husky

Image courtesy of public domain

The answer is B. Alaskan Malamute

Just another way these dogs have shown their usefulness!

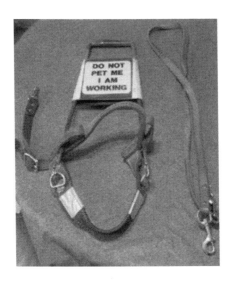

Image courtesy of public domain

Which breed is used for search and rescue, disaster dogs, detection, guide service and therapy?

A. American Bulldog
B. Australian Shepherd
C. Airedale Terrier

Image courtesy of carterse

The answer is B. Australian Shepherd

These dogs are so versatile in what they can do.

Image courtesy of fontplaydotcom

In the 1940's which breed had a dog named "My Own Brucie" that was the most photographed dog in the world?

A. Alaskan Malamute
B. Airedale Terrier
C. American Cocker Spaniel

Image courtesy of RL Johnson

The answer is C. American Cocker Spaniel

My Own Brucie also won the Best in Show at the Westminster Dog Show in 1940 and 1941.

Image courtesy of Highway Patrol Images

Which breed works with customs
agencies for drug detection?

A. Airedale Terrier
B. Australian Cattle Dog
C. Australian Shepherd

Image courtesy of public domain

The answer is B. Australian Cattle Dog

They are also used as service dogs for people with disabilities, therapy dogs, and sometimes as police dogs.

Image courtesy of Joseph A Ferris

Which breed excels at dog sports such as flyball, frisbee, and dog agility?

A. Alaskan Husky

B. Airedale Terrier

C. Australian Shepherd

Image courtesy of Ben Gwilliam

The answer is C. Australian Shepherd

They have strong hips and legs, allowing for fast acceleration and high jumping, sometimes as high as 4 ft.

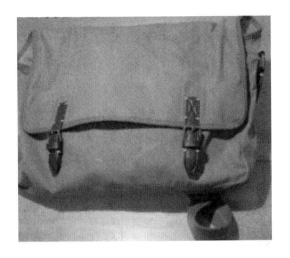

Image courtesy of Lee Cannon

Which breed was used extensively in World War I to carry messages behind enemy lines?

A. Airedale Terrier
B. American Bulldog
C. Australian Shepherd

The answer is A. Airedale Terrier

They also transported mail and were used by the Red Cross to find wounded soldiers on the battlefield.

Image courtesy of Alaskan Dude

Which breed is a highly efficient sled dog?

A. Alaskan Husky

B. Alaskan Malamute

C. Airedale Terrier

Image courtesy of star5112

The answer is A. Alaskan Husky

Huskies win many of the speed-racing events. Winning speeds average more than 19 miles per hour over three days of racing 20-30 miles per day.

Image courtesy of minds-eye

Which breed was used to catch escaped pigs or hunt razorbacks?

A. American Bulldog
B. Australian Cattle Dog
C. Australian Shepherd

Image courtesy of public domain

The answer is A. American Bulldog

Did you know this from hints given earlier in the book?

Congratulations! You can now impress your family and friends with what you know about dog breeds that start with "a".

Look for more quiz books by Wyatt Michaels about other dog breeds, baseball, letter sounds, careers, football, horses, presidents, states, and more.

17720246R00030

Printed in Great Britain
by Amazon